Garbage Delight

Hi Anil! and hi Nigel !

Dennis Lee

Garbage Delight

The poems
were written by
Dennis Lee

The pictures
were drawn by
Frank Newfeld

Macmillan of Canada

A Division of Gage Publishing Limited
Toronto, Canada

for Julian, for Nettie, and for Hugh Kane

Canadian Cataloguing in Publication Data

Lee, Dennis, 1939–
Garbage Delight

ISBN 0-7715-9592-1

I. Newfeld, Frank, 1928–   II. Title.

PS8523.E4G37   jC811'.5'4   C77-001306-6
PR9199.3.L439G37

Originally published in 1977
by The Macmillan Company of Canada
under ISBN 0-7705-1566-5

84 85 86 87 88 89 90 91 92 93 94   A/P   20 19 18 17 16 15 14 13 12 11 10 9 8 7

DESIGN: FRANK NEWFELD

PRINTED AND BOUND IN CANADA BY
ASHTON POTTER LTD.

FOR

MACMILLAN OF CANADA
A DIVISION OF GAGE PUBLISHING LIMITED

Contents

Being Five

I'm not exactly big,
    And I'm not exactly little,
But being Five is best of all
    Because it's in the middle.

A person likes to ride his bike
    Around the block a lot,
And being Five is big enough
    And being Four is not.

And then he likes to settle down
    And suck his thumb a bit,
And being Five is small enough,
    But when you're Six you quit.

I've thought about it in my mind –
    Being Five, I mean –
And why I like it best of all
    Is cause it's In Between.

The Moon

I see the moon
And the moon sees me
And nobody sees
As secretly

Unless there's a kid
In Kalamazoo,
Or Mexico,
Or Timbuktu,

Who looks in the sky
At the end of a day,
And he thinks of me
In a friendly way –

Cause we both lie still
And we watch the moon;
And we haven't met yet
But we might do, soon.

Half Way Dressed

I sometimes sit
    When I'm half way dressed,
With my head in a sweater
    And I feel depressed.

I'm half way out
    And I'm half way in
And my head's nearly through
    But the sweater's gonna win,

Cause the neck-hole grabs
    Like as if it's glue,
And my ears don't like it,
    And my nose don't, too,

And I can't stand sweaters
    When they grab this way,
And they jump on a kid
    And decide to play.

I'm half way dressed,
    And I'm half way dead,
And I'm half way ready
    To crawl back to bed.

Suzy Grew a Moustache

Suzy grew a moustache,
   A moustache,
   A moustache,
Suzy grew a moustache,
   And Polly grew a beard.

Suzy looked peculiar,
   Peculiar,
   Peculiar,
Suzy looked peculiar,
   And Polly looked weird.

Suzy got the garden-shears,
   Garden-shears,
   The garden-shears,
Suzy got the garden-shears
   And Polly got a bomb.

Now Suzy's face is smooth again
   Smooth again,
   Smooth again,
Suzy's face is smooth again,
   And Polly's face is gone.

Inspector Dogbone Gets His Man

Inspector Dogbone
    Is my name
And catching bad guys
    Is my game.

I catch them hot
    I catch them cold
I catch them when they're
    Nine days old

I catch them here
    I catch them there
I catch them in
    Their underwear

I like to catch them
    By the toes
Or by the moustache
    Or the nose

From Corner Brook
    To Calgary
There's not a cop
    Can copy me

Cause every time
    I catch a crook
I hang him up
    On a big brass hook –

Yet here I sit
    In the old Don Jail:
Come gather round
    And I'll tell my tale.

One day, as I
　　Was walking out,
I caught a bad guy
　　By the snout

He robbed a million-
　　Dollar bank
I grabbed his snout
　　And gave a yank

I grabbed his snoot
　　And gave a flick
But then he played
　　A bad-guy trick:

His greasy beak
　　Was big and tough –
But with a snap
　　He bit it off

And just like that
　　His smelly schnozz
Had vanished down
　　His smelly jaws!

At once I grabbed him
　　By the knee:
He ate that too
　　And laughed at me

His neck, his arms,
　　His back, his feet –
Whatever I seized
　　The man would eat

Till all there was
　　Was just a mouth –
Which swallowed itself,
　　And scampered south.

The case was gone!
　　The case was gone!
The nose and the toes
　　And the face were gone!

I had no crook
　　I had no crime
My mighty brain
　　Worked overtime

And figured out
　　A mighty plan
For Dogbone always
　　Gets his man.

I had no crime
　　I had no crook
The only person
　　Left to book

Was one whom I
　　Had long suspected –
Inspector Dogbone,
　　Whom I arrested.

I didn't quake
　　I didn't quail
I threw myself
　　In the old Don Jail

And here I sit
　　Till the end of time,
Easing my soul
　　With a Dogbone rhyme,

The victim of
　　A bad guy's mouth,
Which swallowed itself
　　And scampered south.

But please recall
    As I rot in jail –
Inspector Dogbone
    Didn't fail!

And please remember
    When you can –
Inspector Dogbone
    Got his man!

The Coming of Teddy Bears

The air is quiet
    Round my bed.
The dark is drowsy
    In my head.
The sky's forgetting
    To be red,
And soon I'll be asleep.

A half a million
    Miles away
The silver stars
    Come out to play,
And comb their hair
    And that's OK
And soon I'll be asleep.

And teams of fuzzy
    Teddy bears
Are stumping slowly
    Up the stairs
To rock me in
    Their rocking chairs
And soon I'll be asleep.

The night is shining
    Round my head.
The room is snuggled
    In my bed.
Tomorrow I'll be
    Big they said
And soon I'll be asleep.

The Muddy Puddle

I am sitting
In the middle
Of a rather Muddy
Puddle,
With my bottom
Full of bubbles
And my rubbers
Full of Mud,

While my jacket
And my sweater
Go on slowly
Getting wetter
As I very
Slowly settle
To the Bottom
Of the Mud.

And I find that
What a person
With a puddle
Round his middle
Thinks of mostly
In the muddle
Is the Muddi-
Ness of Mud.

Bigfoot

Bigfoot's sort of Blobby, so he can't exactly Walk,
And he sometimes doesn't answer, cause he does forget his Name,
And he likes to go to School, except he mainly eats the furniture –
    But Bigfoot's like a Terror,
    Bigfoot's like a Tiger,
    Bigfoot's tough as anything in Bad
                            Guy
                                Games!

Suppose that I'm pretending there's a Robber in the bedroom
And he's hiding in the closet, cause he knows I'd Mash him flat,
But he makes a mighty Charge, and he fights me to the window-sill –
    Then Bigfoot's like a Terror!
    Bigfoot's like a Tiger!
    Bigfoot's like a Lion in a Laun-
                      dro-
                          mat!

Or maybe I go out, and I'm being a Detective,
And I think I meet a Midget with a Long Black Veil,
But it isn't him at all, it's a Fat Ferocious Fighting-Freak –
    Then Bigfoot's like a Terror!
    Bigfoot's like a Tiger!
    Bigfoot's like a Jetplane with a Stinger
                          in its
                              Tail!

Bigfoot isn't Pretty, not unless you like the look of him.
Bigfoot isn't Clever, he can barely chew his gum.
But Bigfoot's always There, when there's Rotten kinds of Dangerous
    And Bigfoot's like a Terror!
    Bigfoot's like a Tiger!
    Bigfoot always saves me, so he's Num-
                      ber
                        One!

Then give me some Garbage Delight,
       Right now!
Please pass me the Garbage Delight.

The Snuggle Bunny

The snuggle bunny
    Likes to scrunch
His body up
    In a funny bunch

And wind his teddies
    And his bears
Around and round
    By their soft brown hairs,

And then he burrows
    Like a mole
Inside the nearest
    Snuggle hole

And he snoozles up
    And he snozzles in,
And he goes to sleep
    In his snuggle-down skin.

So if you stumble
    Unawares
On a jumbly clutter
    Of teddy bears,

Unzip the top
    And sort and stir
Through soft brown layers
    Of warm brown fur

And underneath,
    With a faraway roar,
You'll hear a snuggled
    Bunny snore.

"What Will You Be?"

They never stop asking me,
"What will you be? –
A doctor, a dancer,
A diver at sea?"

They never stop bugging me:
"What will you *be*?"
As if they expect me to
Stop being me.

When I grow up I'm going to be a Sneeze,
And sprinkle Germs on all my Enemies.

When I grow up I'm going to be a Toad,
And dump on Silly Questions in the road.

When I grow up, I'm going to be a Child.
I'll Play the whole darn day and drive them Wild.

The Operation

When you walk inside the kitchen
    Very kindly do not shout:
Poor old Hannah's getting mended
    Cause her stuffing all came out.
There's a special dish of ice-cream
    And it's white and brown and red,
And there's cookies if we're quiet,
    Cause we think it hurts her head.

And we never bash old Hannah
    On the floor, except today,
And my Mom has found her needle
    And she thinks she'll be OK;
And old Hannah's pretty brave, she's
    Trying not to cry or scream,
And I'm sorry that I done it
    And I'm having red ice-cream.

When you see the operation
    If you tiptoe you can watch,
Cause her head is feeling better
    But she'll always have a blotch.
And be quiet when you look, and
    Very kindly mind her snout:
My old Hannah's pretty sick, because
    I pulled her stuffing out.

Well, I said I'm awful sorry
    And it wasn't nice to do,
And it might have been on accident
    Except that isn't true,
So I hope that she'll be friends again
    And let me play with her,
Cause she's special to my mind, and now
    I'm going to comb her fur.

The Fly-Nest

I've got a sort of tying thing
    For when I have to tie,
And a box to be a fly-nest
    Cause I'm going to catch a fly.

But I don't exactly get it –
    How you get the fly inside:
Do you open up the lid a bit
    And just go off and hide?

Cause a fly could come along, see,
    And he's looking for a nest,
But he doesn't understand, a box
    Is what a fly likes best.

So he marches up and tells me
    That a box was in the way,
And he rather liked the colour
    But he doesn't care to stay.

And suppose a bigger aminal
    Is walking with his kid,
And he spies a cozy fly-nest
    With a comfy sort of lid,

And they crawl inside, and then the nest
    Is full up to the brim –
And then the fly comes *back*, except
    There isn't room for him!

So I've got to get my tying stuff
    All ready for the plan:
I tell the fly to hurry
    Quick as anybody can,

And *before* those aminals go in
    We catch them round the chest,
And I keep them in my bedroom,
    And the fly can have his nest.

The Bedtime Concert

It's a concert in the bedroom
    With the aminals and toys,
And they think they're making music
    So you mustn't call it noise:
Someone's beating on the bucket
    And he's beat it half to bits
And it's Drumming Monk McGonigle!
    I think he's lost his wits.

And old Hannah's got my trumpet,
    With the wrong end on her snout –
Every time she tries to blow, a sort of
    Sneezy sound comes out;
And the aminals keep playing
    Like as if they never guessed
That the concert in the bedroom
    Isn't what you call the best.

And old Bigfoot's got a whistle, and
    The whistle never stops,
So that every time it doesn't, I could
    Almost call the cops.
But the aminals keep marching
    And they must have marched a mile
And they're all of them so serious
    They make me want to smile.

It's a concert in the bedroom,
    It's a racket in my head,
And pretty soon I'll have to come
    And chase them off to bed.
But they're all my special Aminals,
    Though both my ears are sore,
So I guess I'll let them play for maybe
    Half a minute more.

Goofus

Sometimes my mind is crazy
Sometimes my mind is dumb
Sometimes it sings like angel wings
And beeps like kingdom come.

My mother calls me Mary
My father calls me Fred
My brother calls me Stumblebum
And kicks me out of bed.

Go tell it on a T-shirt
Go tell a TV screen:
My summy's turning tummersaults
And I am turning green.

Don't come to me in April
    Don't come to me in Guelph
Don't come to me in anything
    Except your crummy self.

I haven't got a dollar
    I haven't got a dime
I haven't got a thing to do
    But write these goofy rhymes.

Sometimes my mind is crazy
    Sometimes my mind is dumb
Sometimes it sings like angel wings
    And beeps like kingdom come.

The Secret Song

I've got a secret
    Song I sing
That's secret and special
    As anything.

It's sort of a magical
    Whispery fizz,
But I'm never quite sure
    What the tune part is –

So I jump ahead
    From the stop at the start
To the squeak at the very
    Ending part

Which is actually more
    Of a whistling and dinning,
And everyone thinks
    That it's still the beginning.

And I'm never quite sure
    How the words of it go,
But I just leave them out
    And they don't even show.

And it always works,
    And nobody knows
How my magical, secret
    Sing-song goes.